Emergent-Early Let

MW00999259

Words Their Way

CLASSROOM

 Pearson

Glenview, Illinois   Boston, Massachusetts
Chandler, Arizona   New York, New York

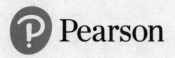

ISBN 13: 978-1-4284-4186-6
ISBN-10:   1-4284-4186-7
3   19

Contents

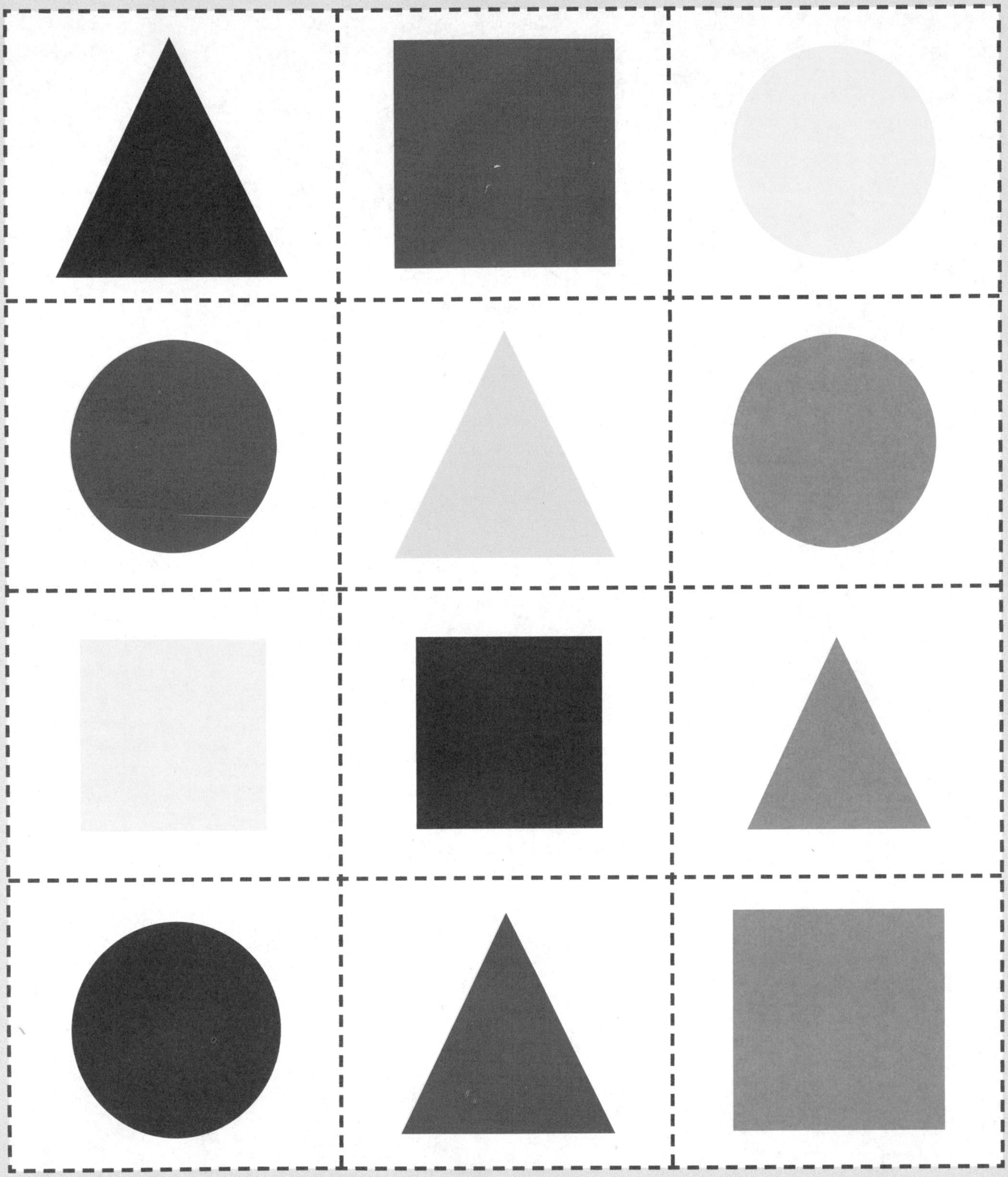

Draw two triangles, two circles, and two squares.

▲	⬤	■

Sort 4: Rhyming Sort Color Words (15)

Draw two sets of things that rhyme.
Write the word below each picture.

Sort 4: Rhyming Sort Color Words

Sort 5: Rhyming Sort Body Parts (19)

Draw a picture that rhymes with nose, a picture that rhymes with knees, a picture that rhymes with hair, and a picture that rhymes with head. Write the word below each picture.

Sort 5: Rhyming Sort Body Parts

Rhyming Sort Pairs

Sort 6: Rhyming Sort Pairs　21

Rhyming Sort Pairs

Draw two sets of things that rhyme.
Write the word below each picture.

Sort 6: Rhyming Sort Pairs

Mm			

Bb			

Sort 7: Beginning Sounds b, m (27)

Draw pictures of two things that begin with Bb and Mm. Write the word below each picture.

Bb	Mm

Sort 7: Beginning Sounds b, m

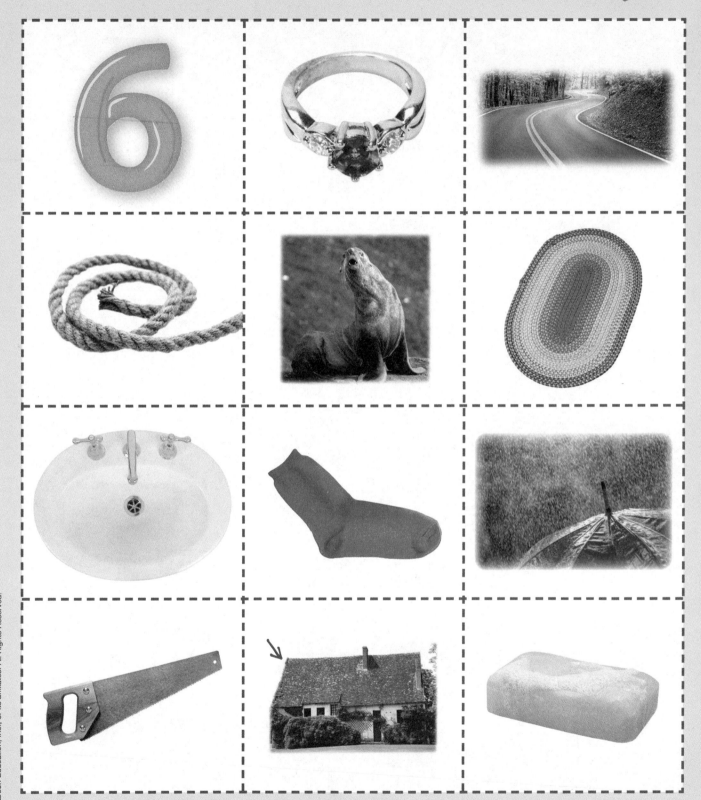

Ss			

Rr			

Draw pictures of two things that begin with
Rr and Ss. Write the word below each picture.

Rr	Ss

Sort 8: Beginning Sounds r, s

Beginning Sounds b, m, r, s

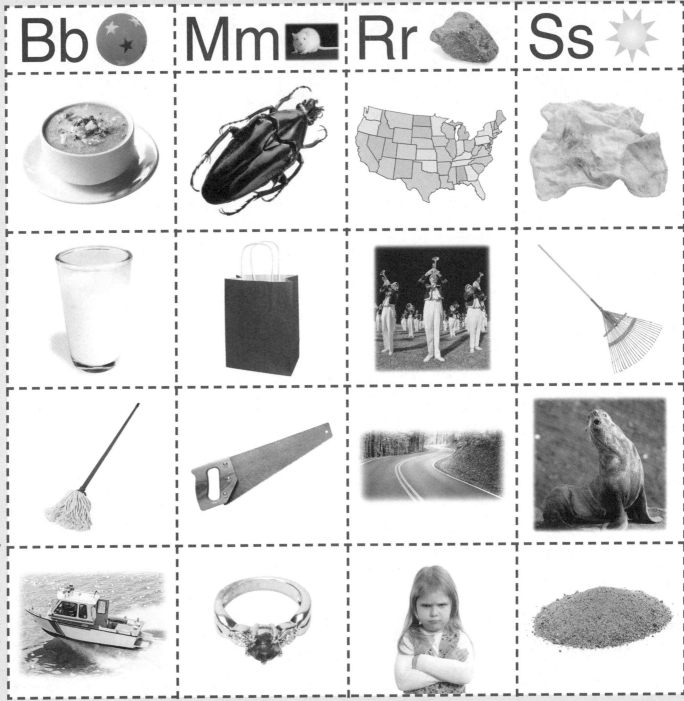

Bb	Mm	Rr	Ss

Draw a picture of one thing that begins with Bb, Mm, Rr, and Ss. Write the word below each picture.

Bb	Mm

Rr	Ss

M	a	b	m
B	A	m	a
M	M	b	B
A	B	M	m
b	B	A	b
a	m	a	A

Aa

Mm

Bb

Say the name of each letter. Then print each letter on the lines.

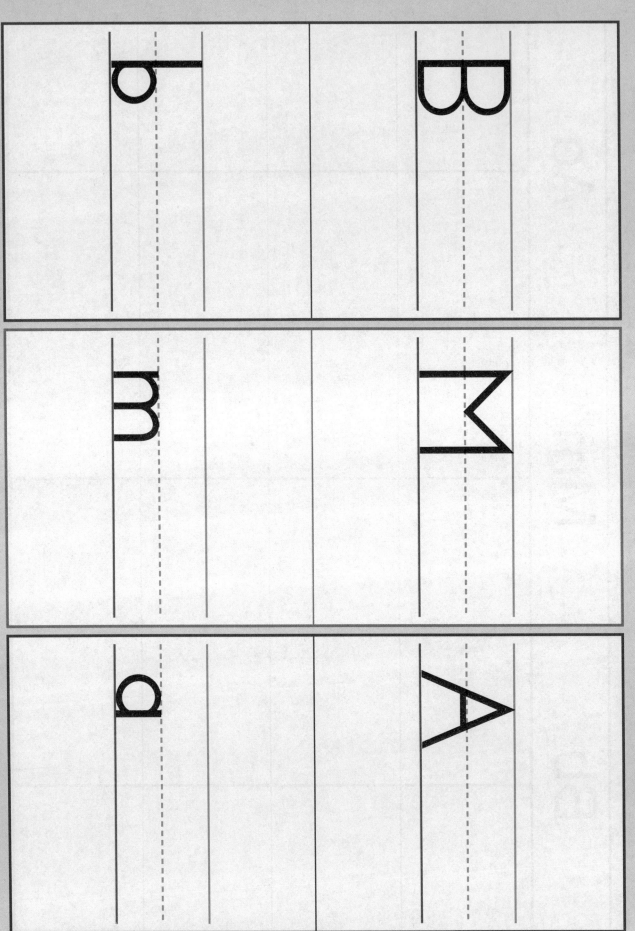

B

b

M

m

A

a

 Sort 10: Letter Recognition Bb, Mm, Aa

E	s	S	S
R	e	R	r
s	E	r	e
S	E	R	s
e	s	E	r
r	e	R	S

Ee

Ss

Rr

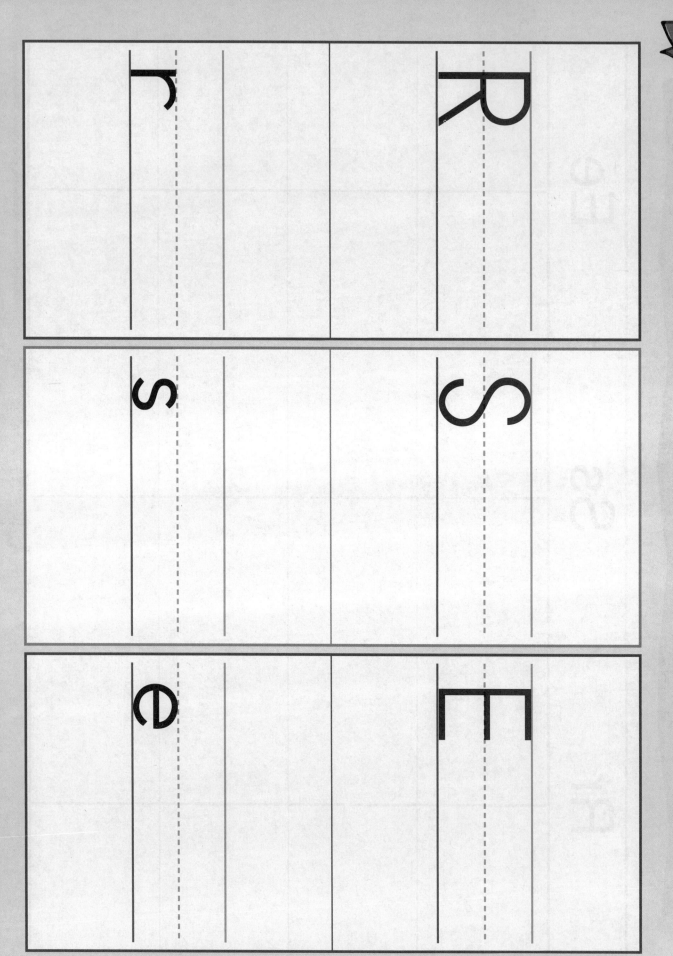

R

r

S

s

E

e

Concept Sort Clothing

Sort 12: Concept Sort Clothing (47)

Draw two things you wear in the winter and two things you wear in the summer. Write the word below each picture.

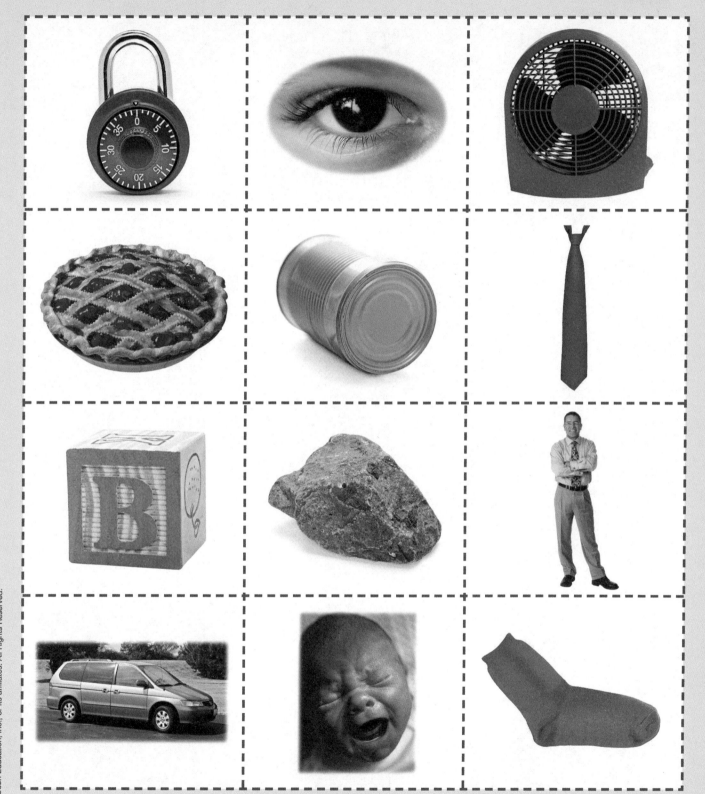

Draw pictures of two things that rhyme with clock, two things that rhyme with fly, and two things that rhyme with pan. Write the word below each picture.

Sort 13: Rhyming Sort Clock, Fly, Pan

Gg

Tt

Draw pictures of two things that begin with
Tt and Gg. Write the word below each picture.

Tt	Gg
_____	_____
_____	_____

Sort 14: Beginning Sounds t, g

Pp

Nn

Sort 15: Beginning Sounds n, p

(59)

Draw pictures of two things that begin with
Nn and Pp. Write the word below each picture.

Nn	Pp
_____	_____
- - - - - - - - - - - - - - -	- - - - - - - - - - - - - - -
_____	_____
_____	_____
- - - - - - - - - - - - - - -	- - - - - - - - - - - - - - -
_____	_____

Sort 15: Beginning Sounds n, p

Tt	Gg	Nn	Pp

Draw a picture that begins with Tt, Gg, Nn, and Pp. Write the word below each picture.

Tt	Gg

Nn	Pp

Syllable Sort Animals

Sort 17

Sort 17: Syllable Sort Animals (65)

Copyright © Pearson Education, Inc., or its affiliates. All Rights Reserved.

Syllable Sort Animals

1	2	3

Draw pictures of two things that have one, two and three syllables. Write the word below each picture.

1	2	3

Sort 17: Syllable Sort Animals

T	g	E	e
E	e	T	t
e	g	t	G
G	E	t	E
t	g	G	T
G	g	T	e

Ee

Gg

Tt

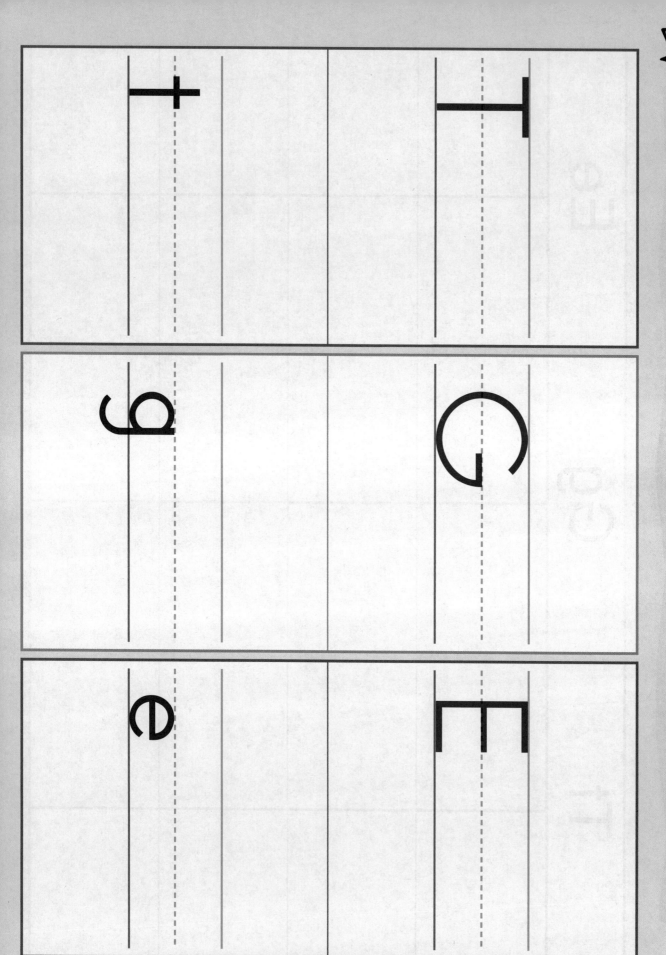

 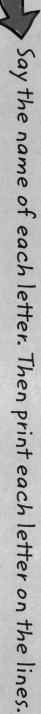

Sort 18: Letter Recognition Tt, Gg, Ee

i	N	P	n
n	p	I	i
I	n	N	p
I	P	p	N
P	n	I	p
i	N	p	i

Ii

Pp

Nn

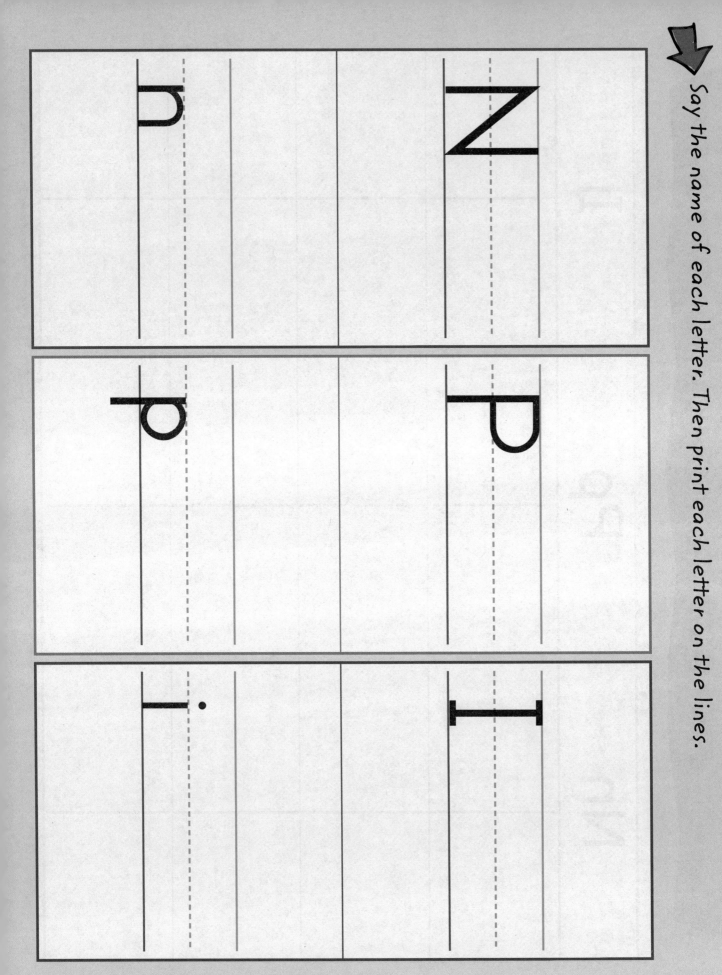

Sort 19: Letter Recognition Nn, Pp, Ii

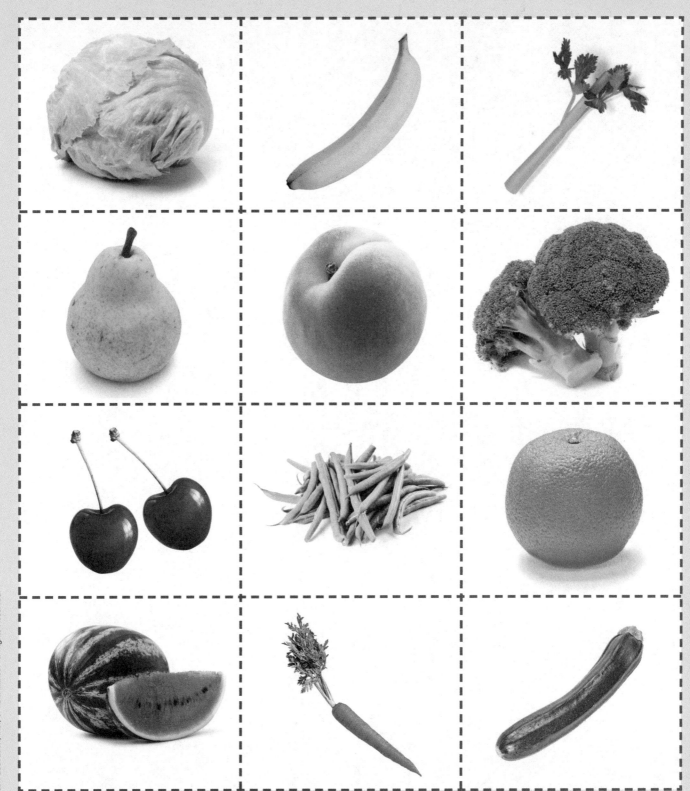

Sort 20: Concept Sort Fruits and Vegetables (77)

Draw two fruits and two vegetables. Write the word below each picture.

Sort 20: Concept Sort Fruits and Vegetables

Beginning Sounds c, h

Hh

Cc

Sort 21: Beginning Sounds c, h 83

Draw pictures of two things that begin with Cc and Hh. Write the word below each picture.

Cc	Hh
_____	_____
_____	_____

Sort 21: Beginning Sounds c, h

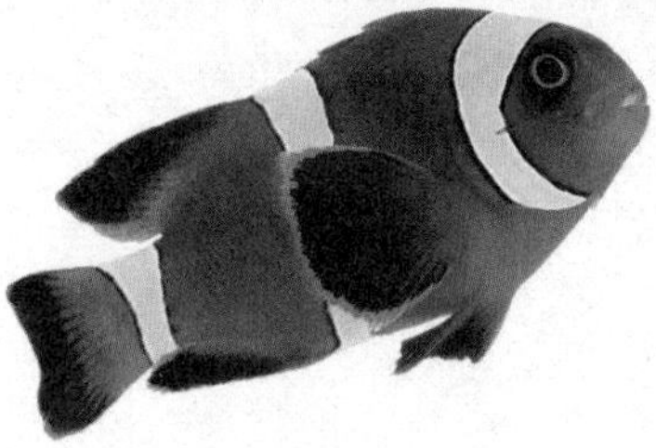
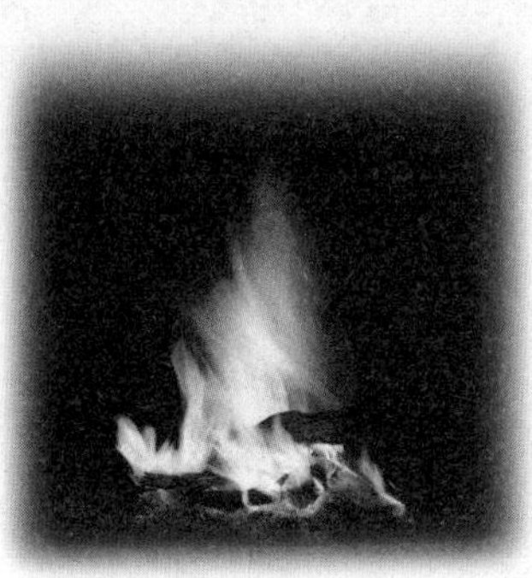
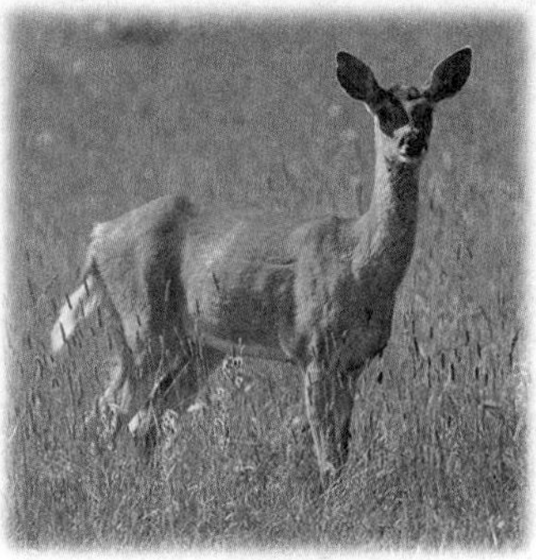
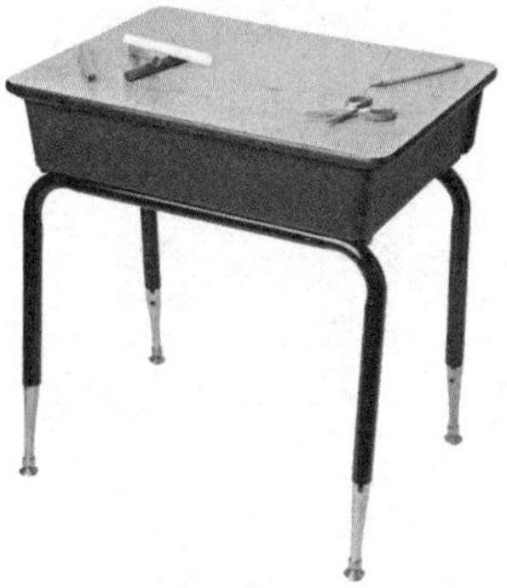
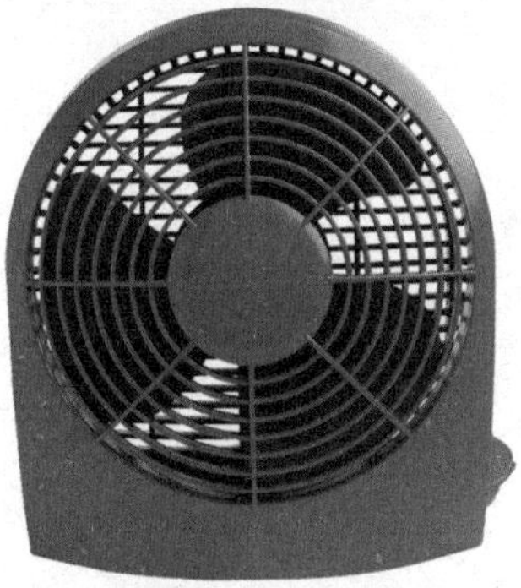
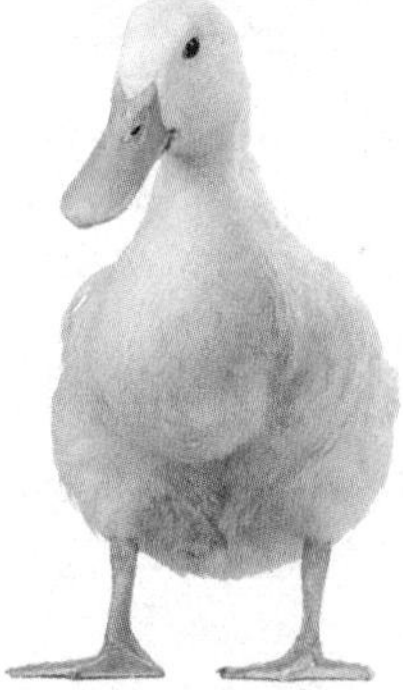
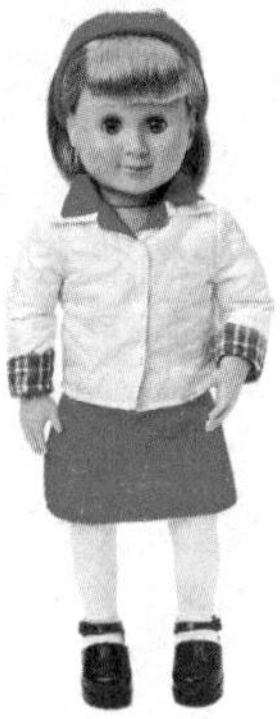
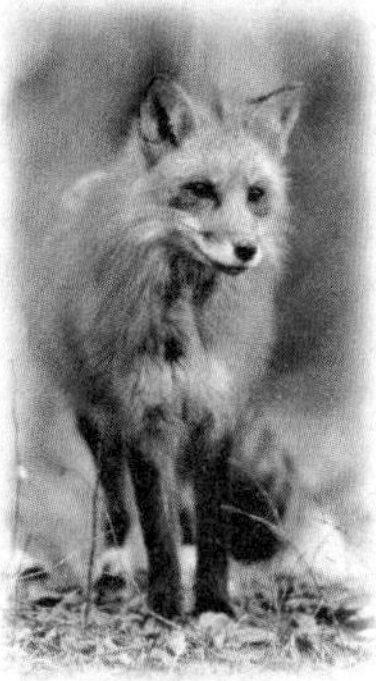
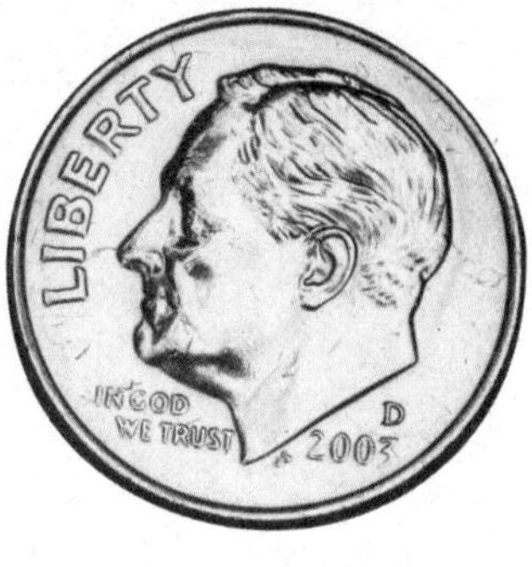
LIBERTY
IN GOD WE TRUST
D
2003
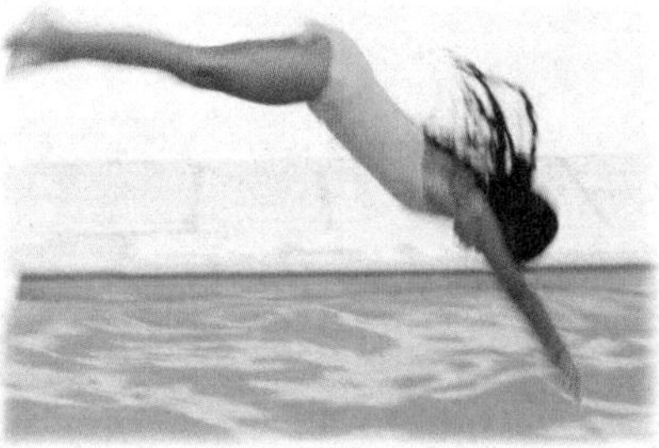
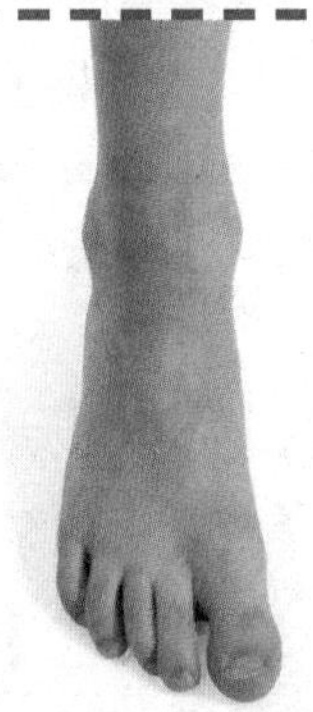
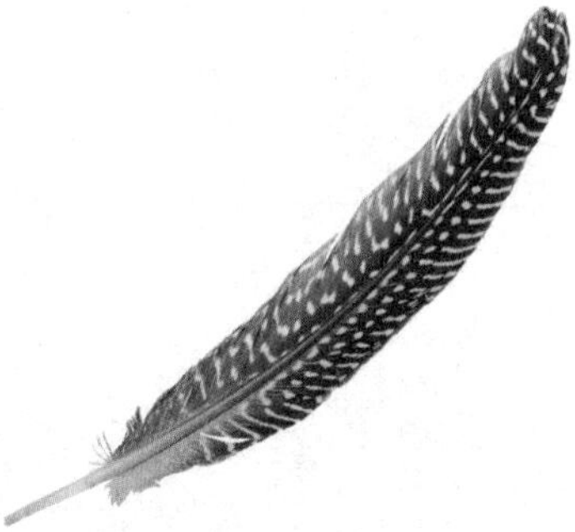

Dd

Ff

Draw pictures of two things that begin with Ff and Dd. Write the word below each picture.

Ff	Dd

Sort 22: Beginning Sounds f, d

Cc	Hh	Ff	Dd

Draw a picture that begins with Cc, Hh, Ff, and Dd. Write the word below each picture.

Cc

Hh

Ff

Dd

Sort 23: Beginning Sounds c, h, f, d

Oddball

Sort 24: Concept Sort Animals and Plants (95)

Draw two animals and two plants. Write the word below each picture.

Sort 24: Concept Sort Animals and Plants

C	h	H	C
C	I	i	h
c	I	H	H
i	h	c	I
i	h	C	i
C	h	I	c

Ii

Hh

Cc

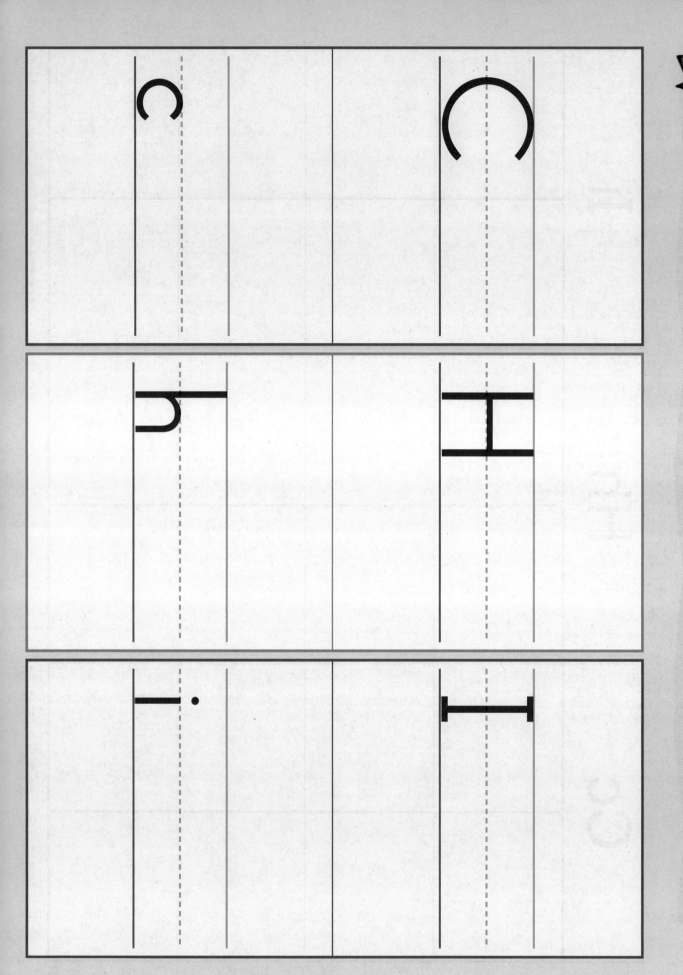

d	F	D	f
d	F	D	A
A	f	F	D
a	A	D	d
A	f	d	F
f	a	d	a

Aa

Dd

Ff

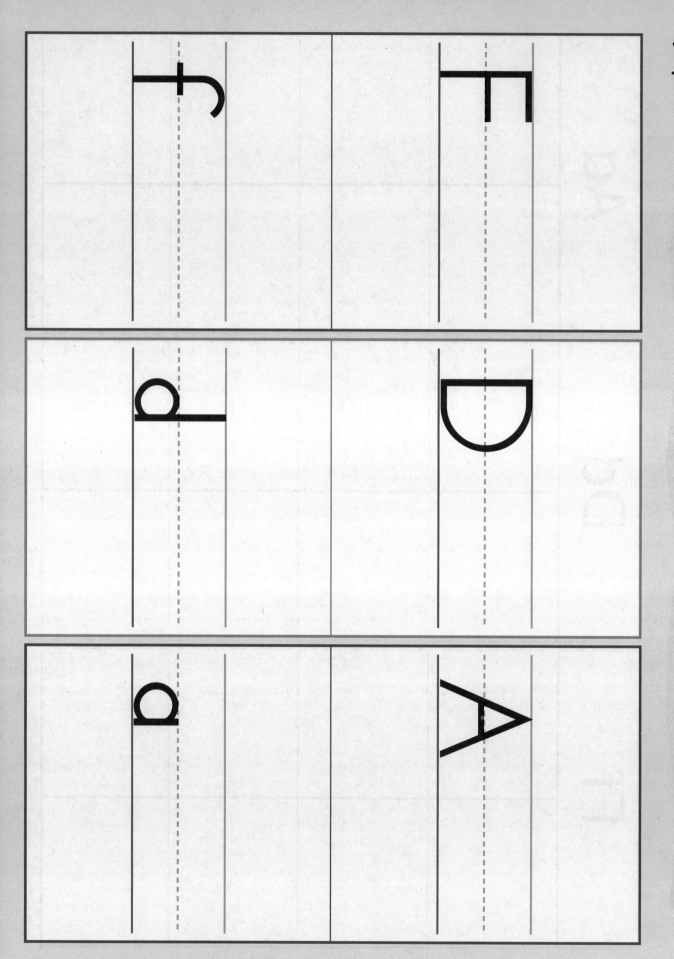

Sort 26: Letter Recognition Ff, Dd, Aa

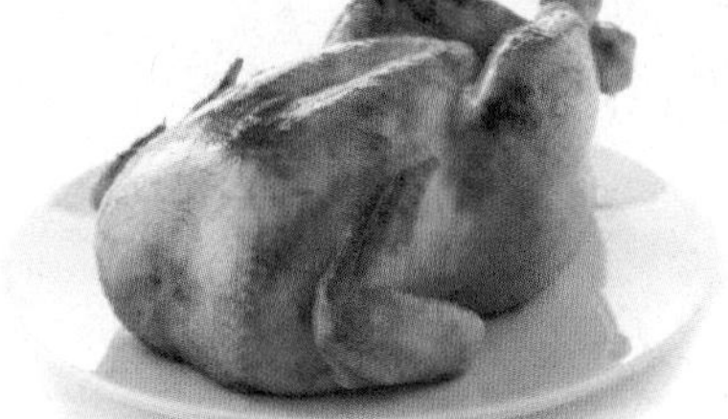

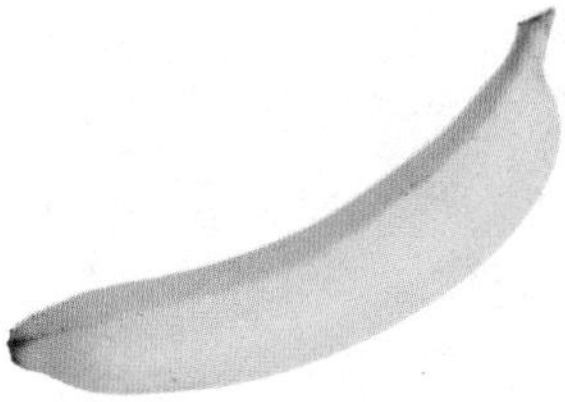

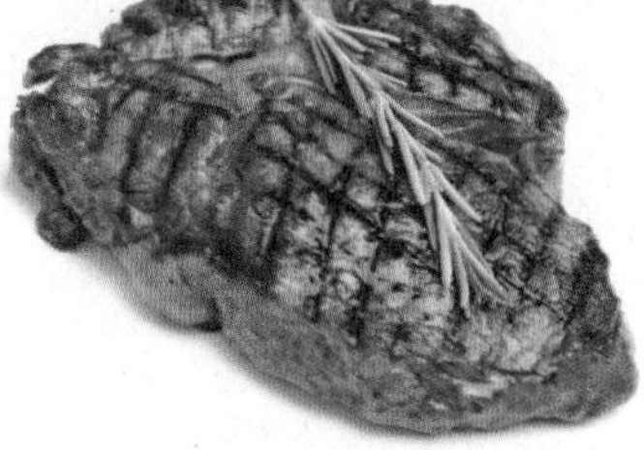

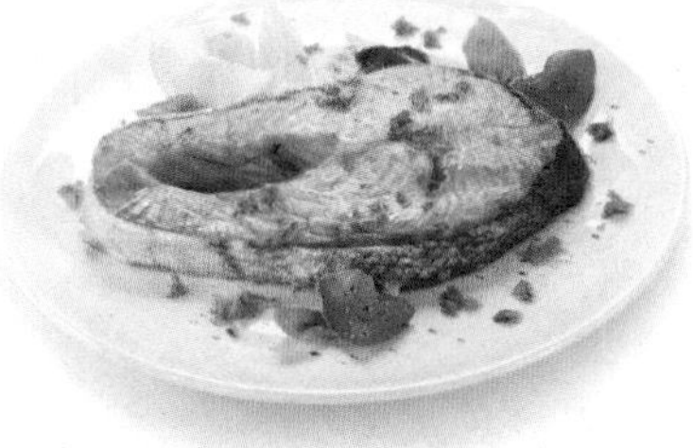

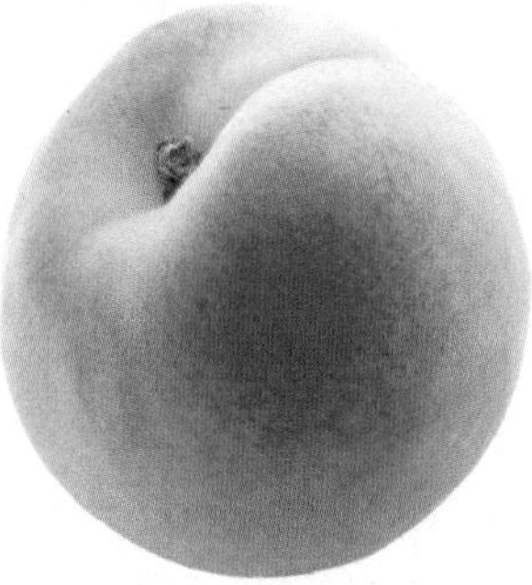

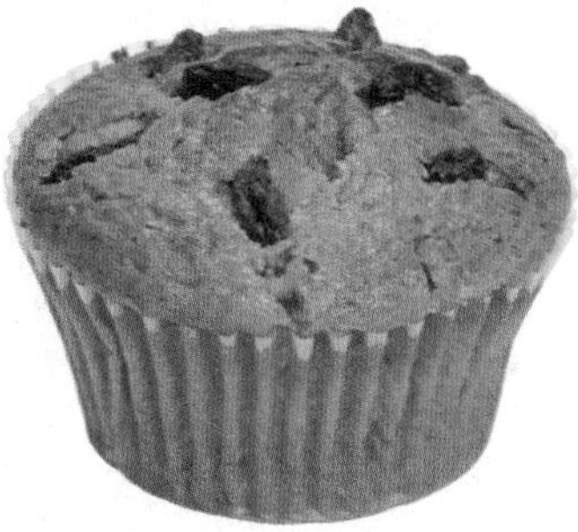

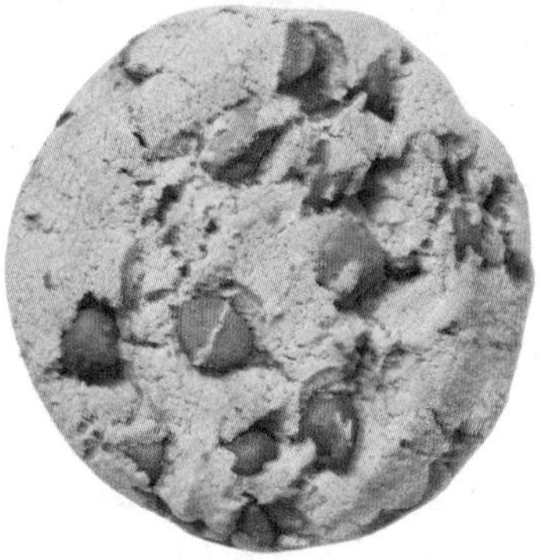

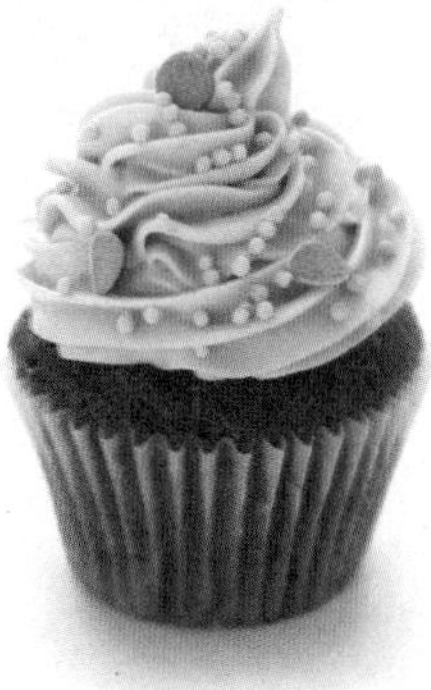

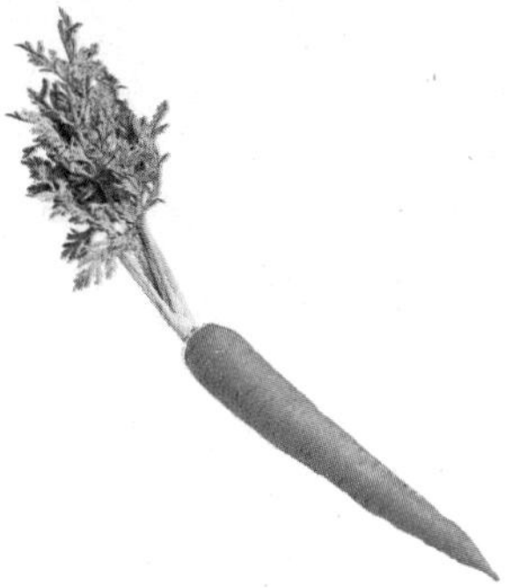

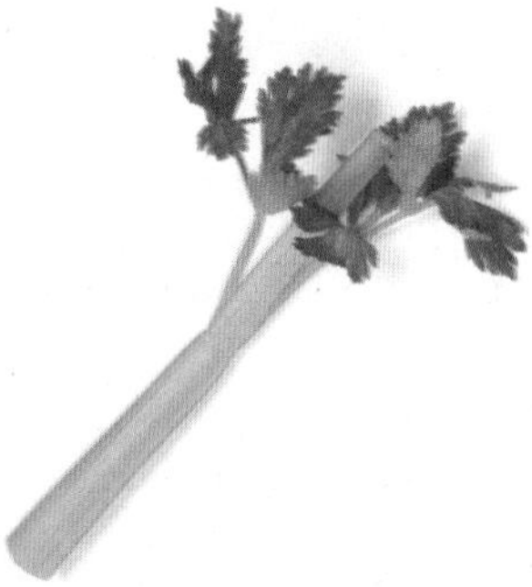

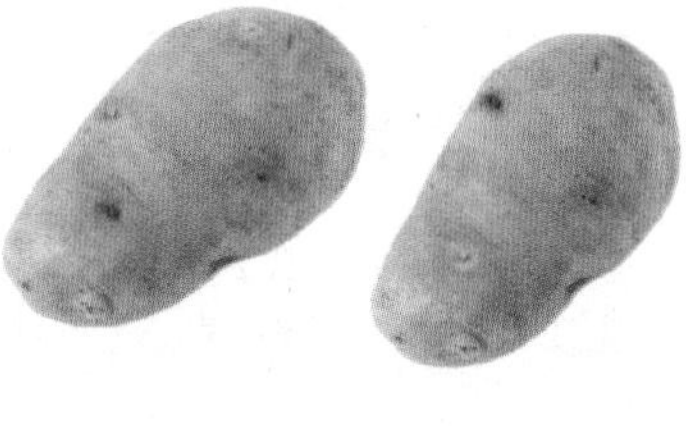

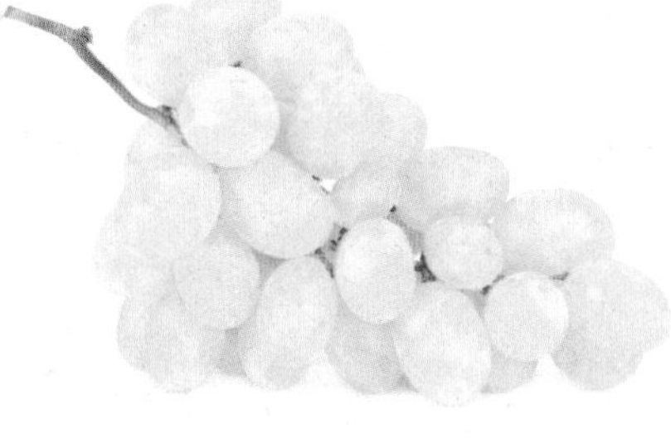

Draw one meat, one bread, one vegetable, and one fruit. Write the word below each picture.

Sort 27: Concept Sort Foods

Kk

Ll

Sort 28: Beginning Sounds l, k (111)

Draw pictures of two things that begin with Ll and Kk. Write the word below each picture.

Ll	Kk

Sort 28: Beginning Sounds l, k

Jj	Ww	Qq

Draw pictures of two things that begin with Jj, Ww, and Qq. Write the word below each picture.

Jj	Ww	Qq

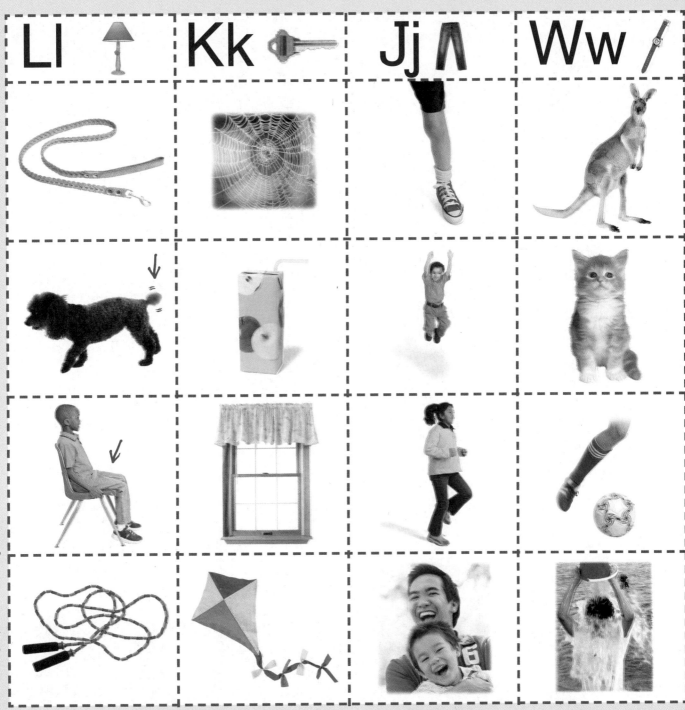

Ll	Kk	Jj	Ww

Draw a picture that begins with Ll, Kk, Jj, and Ww. Write the word below each picture.

Ll	Kk

Jj	Ww

Sort 30: Beginning Sounds l, k, j, w

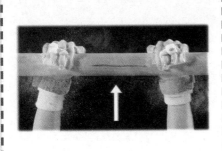

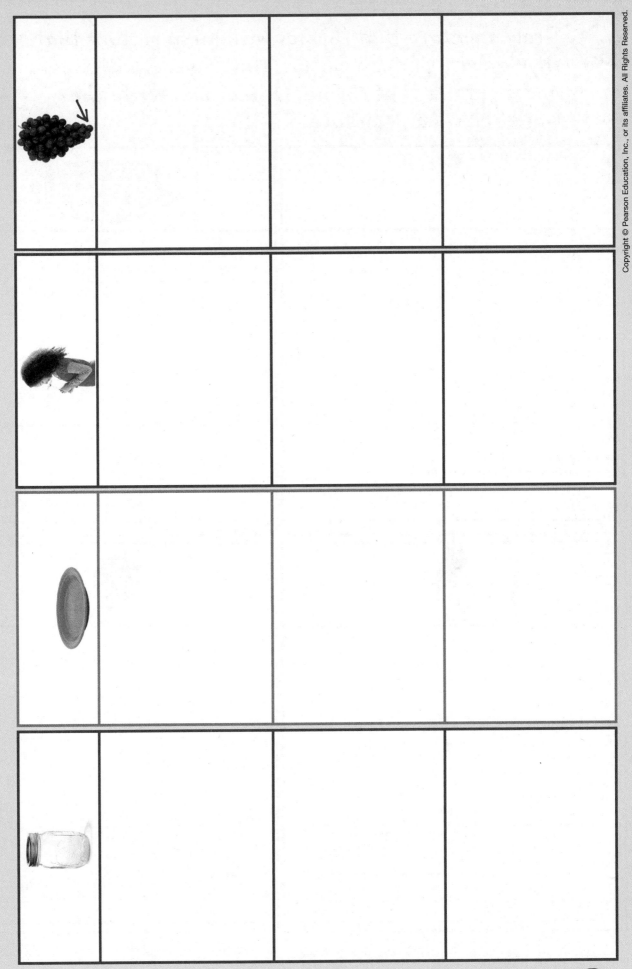

Rhyming Sort Jar, Plate, Smell, Grape

Sort 31: Rhyming Sort Jar, Plate, Smell, Grape (123)

Draw a picture that rhymes with jar, a picture that rhymes with plate, a picture that rhymes with smell, and a picture that rhymes with grape. Write the word below each picture.

Sort 31: Rhyming Sort Jar, Plate, Smell, Grape

Syllables Compound Words

Draw pictures of two things that are compound words. Write the word below each picture.

Concept Sort Cleaning Items

Draw two things for cleaning a person and two things for cleaning the house. Write the word below each picture.

Sort 33: Concept Sort Cleaning Items

K	L	k	K
l	o	O	l
o	L	K	O
L	l	k	l
O	K	o	O
k	L	o	k

Oo

Kk

Ll

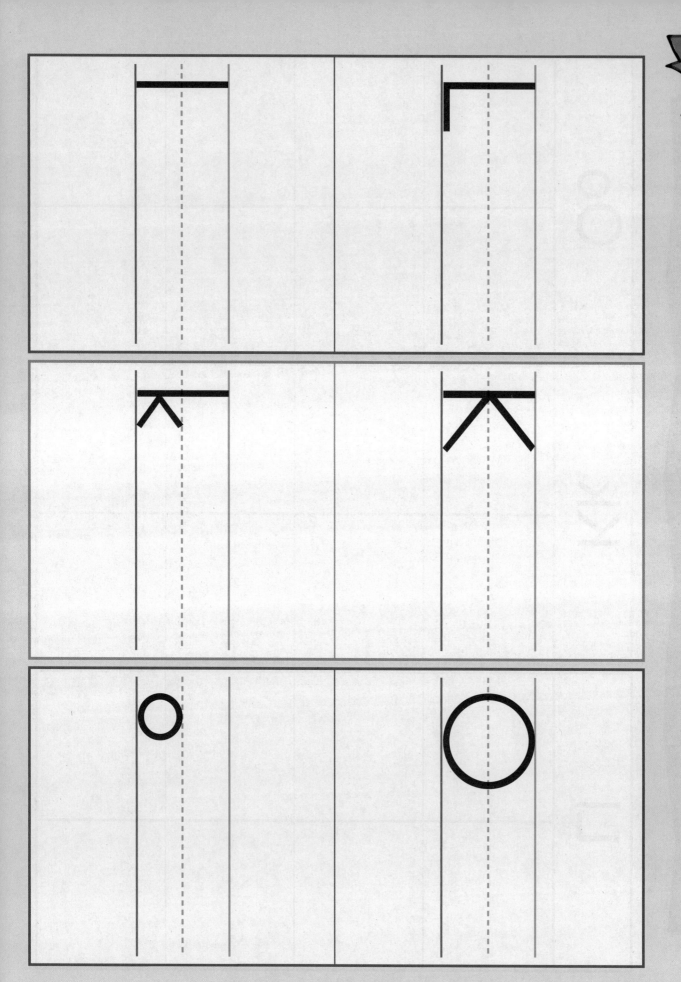

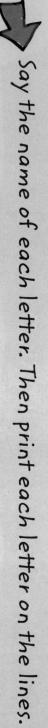

W	J	q	w
j	w	J	j
J	Q	j	Q
q	W	j	w
q	J	W	Q
W	q	Q	w

Qq

Ww

Jj

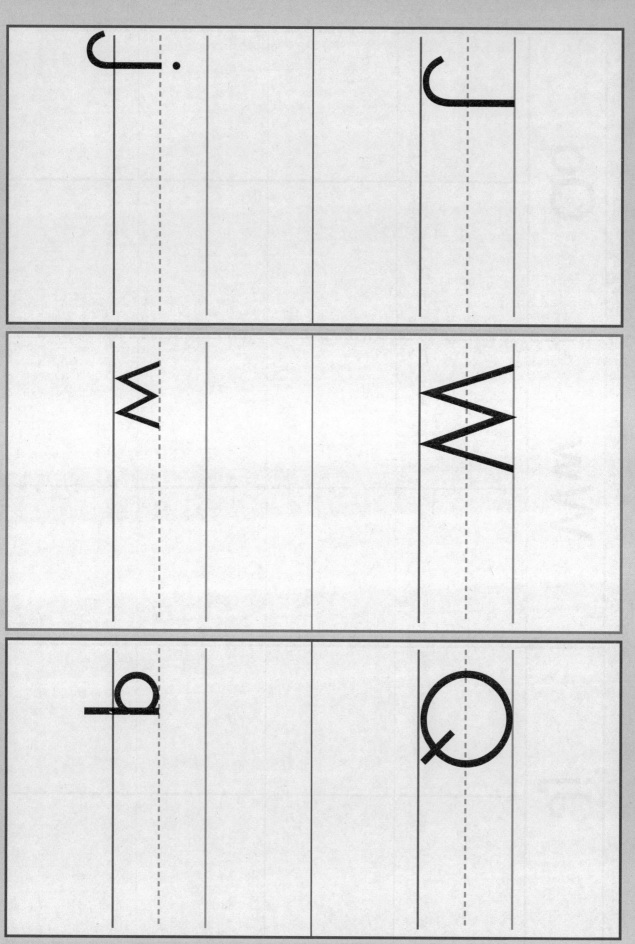

Aa	Bb	Cc	Dd
Ee	Gg	Ii	Jj
Kk	Pp	Qq	Tt
Uu	Vv	Ww	Yy
Zz			

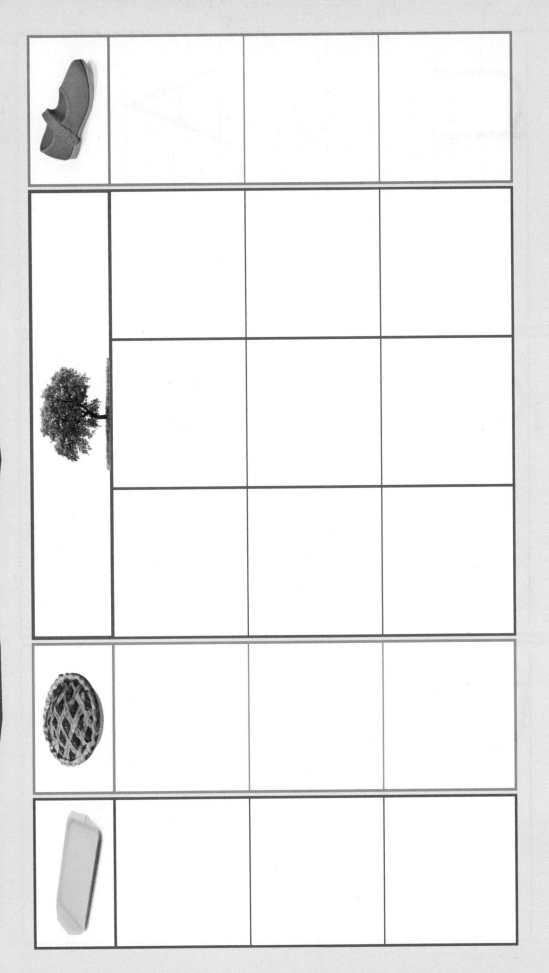

Sort 36: Rhyming Letters (143)

Say the name of each letter. Then print each letter on the lines.

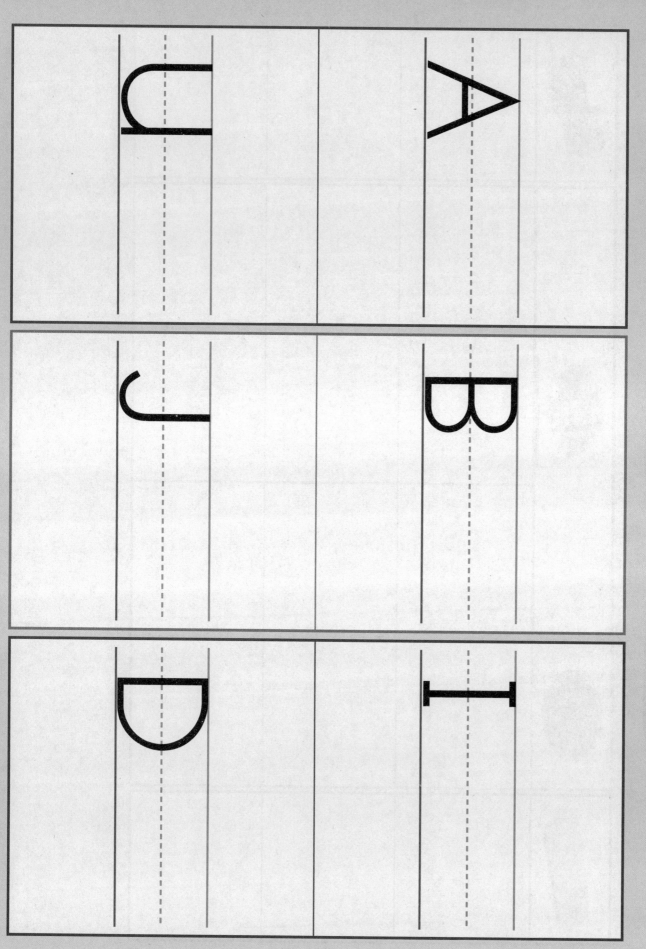

A

B

I

U

J

D

Yy	Zz	Vv

Draw pictures of two things that begin with Yy, Zz, and Vv. Write the word below each picture.

Yy	Zz	Vv

Sort 37: Beginning Sounds y, z, v

Ending Sounds t, x

Sort
38

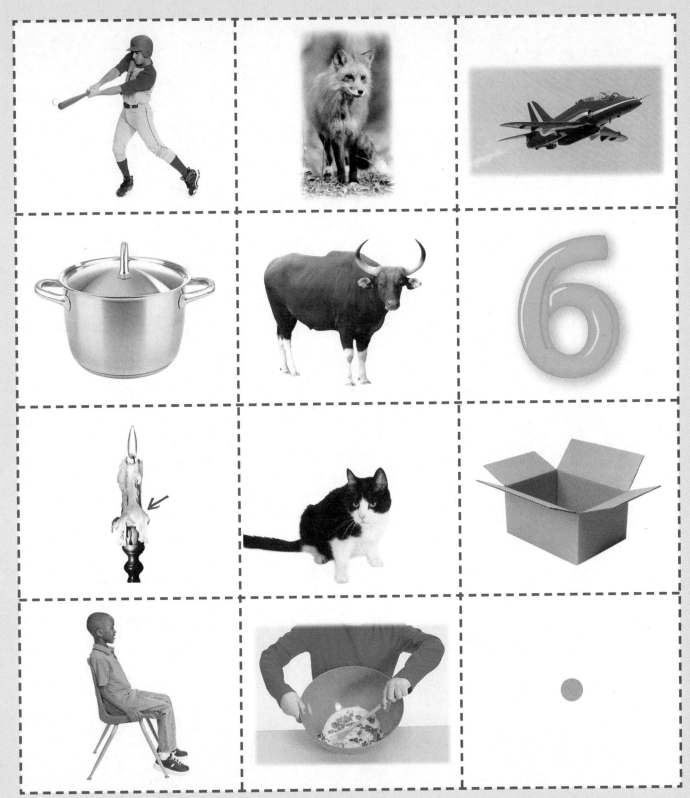

ax

bat

Draw pictures of two things that end with Tt and Xx. Write the word below each picture.

bat	ax

y	Z	v	Y
Z	y	V	Z
v	Z	Y	V
Y	V	z	Z
z	y	v	Y
V	Z	Y	v

Vv

Zz

Yy

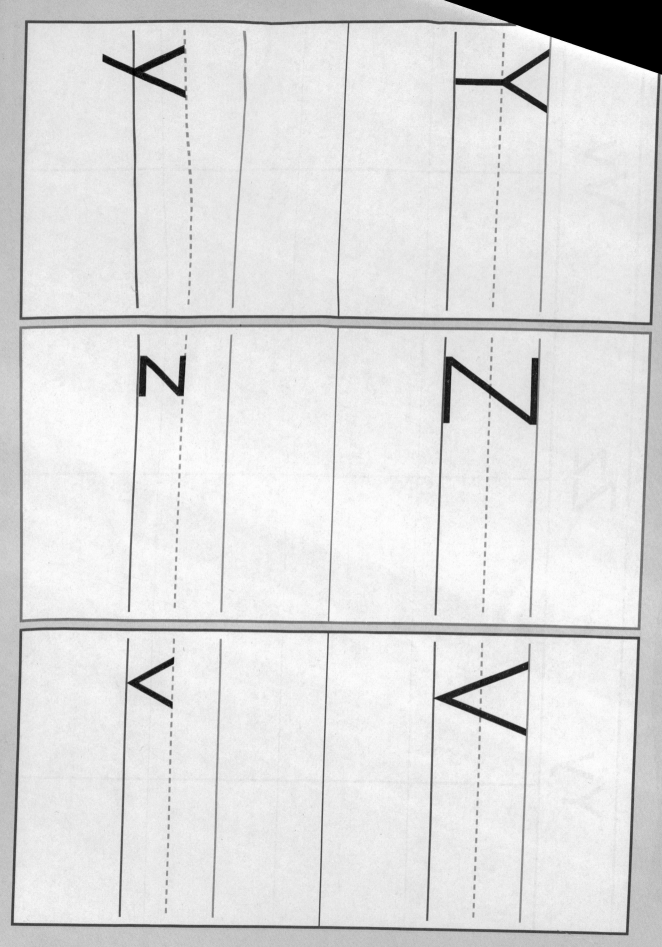

Sort 39: Letter Recognition Yy, Zz, Vv

t	U	x	t
u	t	X	U
x	U	T	X
T	X	u	u
u	t	x	T
X	U	T	X

Uu

Xx

Tt

Say the name of each letter. Then print each letter on the lines.

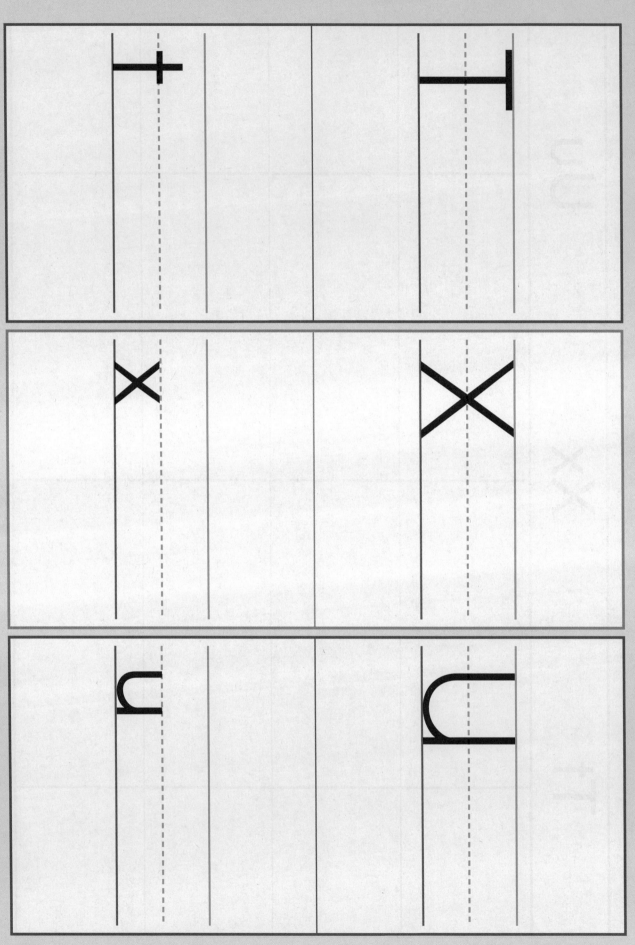

Say the name of each picture. Circle the two pictures whose names rhyme.

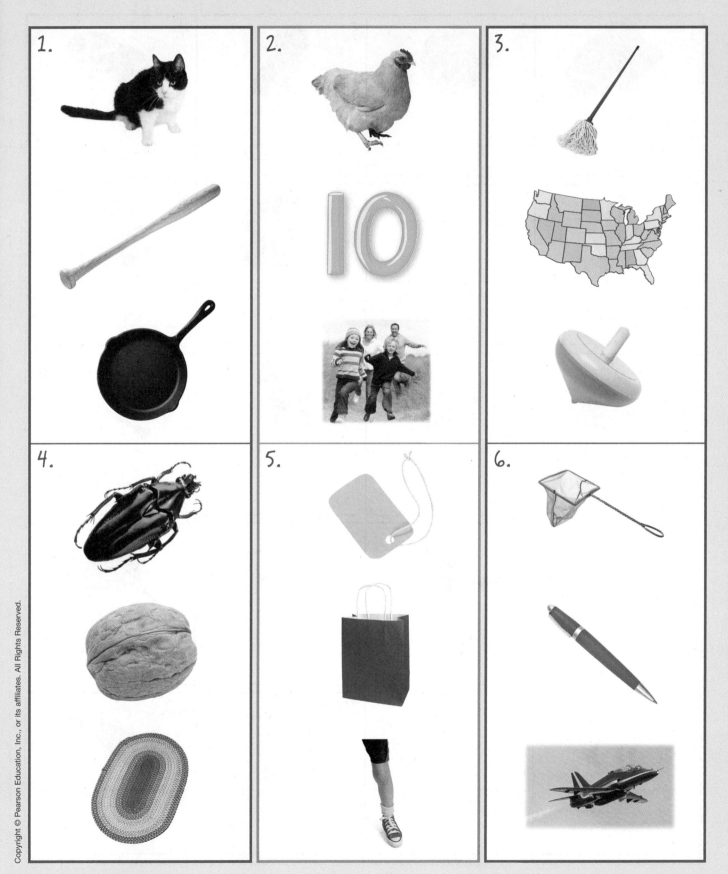

Say the name of each picture. Write the capital and lowercase letter that stands for the beginning sound.

1.	2.	3.	4.
5.	6.	7.	8.
9.	10.	11.	12.
13.	14.	15.	16.
17.	18.	19.	20.

Spell Check 2: Beginning Consonants

Say the name of each picture. Write the capital and lowercase letter that stands for the beginning sound.

1.	2.	3.	4.
5.	6.	7.	8.
9.	10.	11.	12.
13.	14.	15.	16.
17.	18.	19.	20.

Spell Check 3: Beginning Consonants   163

Write the matching letter next to each letter shown.

1. A

2.

3. B

4. g

5. T

6. e

7.

8. K

9. L

10. y

11. J

12. Q

13. r

14. I

15. m

16. f

17. V

18.

19. D

20. X

16. h

18. p